The Wonder Works Workbook

FIRST EDITION

© 2020 by Noelle Federico with Toni Stone

All rights reserved. No part of this book may be reproduced without the permission in writing from the author, except by a reviewer who may quote brief passages in a review with appropriate credit; nor may any part of this book be reproduced, stored in a retrieval system, or transmitted in any form or by any means-electronic, photocopying, recording or other- without permission in writing from the publisher.

For information or permissions write:

Wonder Works Studio LLC
P.O. Box 342, Fairfax, VT 05454

www.wonderworksstudio.com

Publisher: Wonder Works Studio LLC

Cover Design by Creative Pear www.creativepear.net
Back Cover Photo by Tia Rooney Photography, Fairfax, VT

ISBN# 978-1-7359355-0-8

Thank you...

God... for all the blessings, the Grace and for always making ways where there are no ways.

Mom...you will always be my sunshine... ti amo di più

To my followers, supporters and fans of **The Working Single Mom** brand and your children, thank you for allowing me into your lives and thank you for every day pushing me to work harder and be better so that I will have insights to share with you...you are all MY inspiration...

For Mom...

In My Life by The Beatles...

There are places I'll remember

All my life, though some have changed

Some forever, not for better

Some have gone, and some remain

All these places had their moments

With lovers and friends, I still can recall

Some are dead, and some are living

In my life, I've loved them all

But of all these friends and lovers

There is no one compares with you

And these memories lose their meaning

When I think of love as something new

Though I know I'll never lose affection

For people and things that went before

I know I'll often stop and think about them

In my life, I'll love you more

Though I know I'll never lose affection

For people and things that went before

I know I'll often stop and think about them

In my life I'll love you more

In my life I'll love you more

***Source: LyricFind

Songwriters: John Lennon / Paul McCartney

In My Life lyrics © Sony/ATV Music Publishing LLC

Introduction

If you are new to my work, welcome. If you have been following me through time, welcome back. On August 26th, 2020 at approx. 2am my Mother exited this world...she had prepared me as much as possible for this development although it varied greatly from our original plan that she would live to be 99 (she passed at 75).

Lately, I have been asking myself how I can use her work and my own to make the biggest impact given the platforms that I have at my disposal---I decided to start creating additional content suitable for younger folks too--as they ARE the future and if I can help them see that they have everything to do with how their lives turn out then I will have used my life wisely.

My Mother taught success and prosperity principles for over 4 decades and she published about 40 books. Wonder Works Studio LLC will continue its tradition of teaching and publishing material that helps people and now children to improve the quality of their lives.

She named her company Wonder Works Studio because she said that "wondering" works---when you wonder about things it helps you learn and be open to new possibilities.

This workbook is designed to be simple enough to use with your children as well as you can use it yourselves...I have included quotes written in my Mother's original hand (she was also a graphic artist) as well as collections of her affirmations that you may find helpful.

She was the original 'working single mom' that inspired me to create this brand back in 2014—she began teaching me these tools and principles when I was 11. Her original work began with children as she was the Art Director for the Boys Clubs of Boston where she created a program called 'Shared Summer'...

Her wish was that I continue to coach, teach, write and share our work with as many people as possible hence this workbook.

My intention is that both you and your children will understand that in your lives the power lies with you--- when you learn to focus and manage your mind ALL things are possible.

I wish for you every good and wonderful thing.

Much Love to you all,

Noelle

Fairfax, VT

October 24, 2020

Wonder:

won·der

as a noun

a feeling of surprise mingled with admiration, caused by something beautiful, unexpected, unfamiliar, or inexplicable.

as a verb

desire or be curious to know something.

I GET JUST WHAT I EXPECT

... i believe
it's possible
that's how come
i get it...

www.wonderworks.org / wonder works studio   buck hollow road   fairfax, VT.
05454

Welcome to The Wonder Works Workbook—I hope you have as much fun filling it out as I did creating it for you!

Please use this workbook to help you understand that you have the ability and power to change anything in your life that you don't like. Sometimes changing things means to change the way that we LOOK at things---for example if you don't like your school or your job and you complain about it all the time instead you could start to find small things that you DO like and talk about those instead.

When we complain about things and are in a bad mood all the time we are like that character 'Pig Pen' from Charlie Brown who always has a dirt cloud around his head---that dirty cloud follows him wherever he goes.

When we focus on what is wrong and what we don't like we make a cloud around us that brings everything down...it's almost like we are spreading dirt everywhere we go.

Doing this makes it REALLY hard for good things and good ideas to find you. Focusing on what IS going right and being kind to people, helping people and looking for the GOOD are all things that make a cloud of light around us and then we naturally attract amazing things right TO US.

People think it is a miracle---the truth is that YOU can make your own miracles by learning to train your mind to focus. I am going to give you some tools to help you do just that.

Let's start by looking at the past year as it closes out, this was a very strange year for everyone in the whole world and it will be good for us to take a closer look at it...start to think about what happened this year ---what should be celebrated, what you want to leave behind you, the blessings, the things you learned...there is a lot of power in evaluating something and saying it is 'complete' which means you are finished with it!

Lots of times we are so busy just trying to just 'get through it' that we forget to really LOOK at what happened…so take some time and let's help you to be complete with this year…

- **What were you happy about this year?**

- **What made you sad or uncomfortable this year?**

- **What did you do that you were proud of this year?**

"Change in attitude doesn't happen overnight."

—bri stone

- **What did you wish you had done this year that did not get done?**

- What were the BEST things that happened to you this year?

- **What were some BIG things you learned this year?**

- What habits or behaviors do you want to leave behind as you finish off this year?

- As you think about the New Year, what attitudes do you want to leave behind?

- What is the MOST important thing that happened this year? How did it make you feel?

- **What is worth celebrating from this year?**

- **What do you need help to not repeat this year?**

- Rate this past year on a scale of 1 to 10--- 10 being the BEST

- What word best describes/ sums up this year?

Okay, good work everybody!!!! ...take one last look over your end of year wrap-up and then let's bless it ALL...the lessons, the hard stuff, the celebrations...all of it. Now declare yourself complete, forgiving yourself for all the things that you think you could have done better. Accept that you did the best you could and it was all perfect. Now time to move on to what's next... creating a WONDERFUL New Year!!!

"Getting people to like you... is only the other side of liking them."

— Norman Vincent Peale

Here are TWO things that are going to help you create the NEW year that you want:

1. <u>Affirmation Flash Cards</u>

    If you are an adult you will remember flash cards from when you were a kid and if you are younger than an adult maybe you have used flash cards in school to learn something. When I was in school, we used them to train ourselves to learn information such as multiplication tables or the periodic table of elements...

    Now we are going to use them to alter the way that you think about your life. Start by getting 10 index cards and on each card write an affirmation or statement of how you want your life to be.

    - Examples:
        - I do well in school.
        - I have many good friends.
        - I am healthy and happy.
        - I am well paid with plenty of money to spare and share.
        - I workout daily and eat only foods that serve me.
        - My relationships contribute to my life.
        - My children are happy and healthy.
        - I have plenty of energy to do what needs to be done by me.

    ***at the end of this book there are lots of affirmations that you may find helpful as you begin using this tool.

You get the idea…once you have your 10 statements then use the cards twice a day, flipping through them until the statements on them become part of the way that you think about your life. Change/update the cards as needed.

2. <u>Choose Your Words Wisely</u>

   Your words have a LOT more power than you think they do…stop complaining, stop talking about what you don't want more of, speak about things based on how you want them to be and not on the way that they look in the moment.

   Remember the example I gave earlier about the dirt cloud—if you cannot find something good or positive to say just be quiet for a while. Complaining, whining and being nasty or negative only makes the day worse for everyone.

   <u>You will create what you speak about</u>—so make sure that you are speaking about the good and about what you want to see happen. Do not use your words to spread doom and gloom.

- What are some NEW habits that you want to create this year?

- **What do you want to accomplish this year?**

- What are some NEW things that you want to learn this year? How about something NEW that you want to try?

- **What are you going to do this year to take care of yourself?** (ex. eat healthier, drink more water, do yoga, ride your bike more, get outside for walks, roller skate)

- What can you do to be a better HELPER? Where can you make a difference by helping others?

- **How can you be a better friend?**

- **What is the ABSOLUTE best thing about you?**

•What do you want to change this year?

"TO FEAR IS TO BELIEVE SOMETHING THAT YOU DO NOT WISH (INTEND) TO BELIEVE"

—helen wilmans

- **What would you do if you could not fail?**

- If you were a Superhero what would your name be? What would your superpower be??

- **What do you want people know about you?**

- **Who would you like to spend more time with this year?**

> "For everything you missed, you gained something else."
>
> – Ralph Waldo Emerson

- Who do you want to be when you grow up?

Why?

How can you be more like that NOW?

- My biggest fear is

- What I really want to do is

- If I could make a living doing whatever I wanted, I would

- I like people who

- My favorite thing in the world is

- Do you let being afraid of something stop you from doing it?

- What if this year you did it anyway----what if you felt afraid and did it anyway? What do you think would happen?

it's not what we have in our life, but **WHO** we have in our life THAT COUNTS.

—J.M. Laurence

wonder works studio buck hollow rd. fairfax, Vermont

- What are the 5 things that you appreciate MOST about yourself?

- What is your WORD for this NEW year?

- **What are you excited about for this year?**

•What are you grateful for RIGHT NOW?

Goal Setting/ Manifestation List

When you want to create something or when you have a goal that you want to bring into being it is a good idea to get into the habit of writing down what you want to manifest.

Writing these things down on a consistent basis and reviewing them frequently helps your mind to bring them into your life.

When you write something down in your own handwriting it helps you to OWN it—meaning that it helps you to imagine it and that helps make it real for you.

After you write down the things that you want, look at the list regularly and every month cross off the things that happened and list out new things that you want to happen.

Use the monthly sheets to keep track of your lists and at this time next year you will be surprised at all the progress you have made!

Here are some definitions to help you understand the words manifest and goal.

Goal: a result that you want to achieve

        ex. to be on the Honor Roll at school

Manifest: to prove, to show plainly, to bring into being

January 2021

My Goals for this Month:

Action Steps that I need to take:

What I want to manifest this month:

February 2021

My Goals for this Month:

Action Steps that I need to take:

What I want to manifest this month:

March 2021

My Goals for this Month:

Action Steps that I need to take:

What I want to manifest this month:

April 2021

My Goals for this Month:

Action Steps that I need to take:

What I want to manifest this month:

May 2021

My Goals for this Month:

Action Steps that I need to take:

What I want to manifest this month:

June 2021

My Goals for this Month:

Action Steps that I need to take:

What I want to manifest this month:

July 2021

My Goals for this Month:

Action Steps that I need to take:

What I want to manifest this month:

August 2021

My Goals for this Month:

Action Steps that I need to take:

What I want to manifest this month:

September 2021

My Goals for this Month:

Action Steps that I need to take:

What I want to manifest this month:

October 2021

My Goals for this Month:

Action Steps that I need to take:

What I want to manifest this month:

November 2021

My Goals for this Month:

Action Steps that I need to take:

What I want to manifest this month:

December 2021

My Goals for this Month:

Action Steps that I need to take:

What I want to manifest this month:

WHAT IS REQUIRED IS ALWAYS PRESENT

COUNT ON THIS

..... principles 16 to 20

Creating a Vision Board

Using your imagination is a powerful tool—being able to picture the things that you want to create for your future helps you to bring them into your life. Making a vision board is a fun and creative way to do that. Below are the materials needed and some simple guidelines to get you started. Have fun!

MATERIALS that you will need:

- Poster board
- Magazines
- Other images and text from artwork, old books, computer printouts, etc. (optional)
- Scissors
- Glue sticks or rubber cement glue
- Paper and pen
- Sharpies or other permanent markers (optional)

- The first thing to do is to make a list of the areas that you might want to cover on your board—things like income/money, health, relationships, family, school, work, skills, travel, creativity etc. Once you have an idea of the areas that you want to cover you will know what kinds of pictures and words you are looking for.

- Find images and words for the vision board. Search for and cut out images and words that represent your goals and/or the things that you want to manifest for your future. Go through stacks of magazines and clip everything you like—colors, words, interesting images—that relate to your goals and intentions.

- Next, sort and arrange the images and words that you feel best represent the goals and intentions that you have in mind for yourself. Once you are happy with the arrangement you can glue the words and pictures onto the poster board. You can add your own words if you wish either in your handwriting or by typing things out on the computer and printing them out. Save the pictures and words that you don't use (start a folder) because you may use them next time. This vision board process is one that you will want to repeat every few months as your intentions and goals will change and you will want to keep it fresh.

- Display your board on the wall in your bedroom where you will be able to look at it several times a day---every time you look at it say to yourself,

    "every day in every way things are getter better and better"

End Note...

To create a future unlike the past takes work, you need to put in the effort to have the kind of life that you want. ANYTHING is possible if you are willing to do the work.

Use the index cards, pay attention to how you are using your words, write down your goals and the things you want to manifest and create your vision boards. Look at them several times a day. Go over your goals/ manifestation list daily and make new lists monthly---change out your index cards when needed. These things are TOOLS—tools are meant to be used.

The only person that can say how your life turns out is you, no matter what your circumstances are you still have power over your own words, thoughts and actions. In order to change your life you have to be able to control yourself and stay focused on your intentions.

The world will constantly be trying to draw your attention to what is wrong and what isn't working--- you must be able to FOCUS on what is important to you.

No matter how old you are you CAN change your life, you only need to do the work and it IS work. Every day you have to remember to be happy and grateful, you have to leave complaining and whining at the door. Use the tools, do the work and email me to tell me how you are doing.

You can reach me at noelle@fortunatopartners.com and I actually read my own emails:) and I respond.

I know the world seems crazy right now, however it is only what it looks like in the moment. This too shall pass and the more you can stay focused on the good and the life that you want to have the better off you will be. Everything turns out. I promise.

When I was 11, Mom taught me to constantly repeat to myself, "every day in every way things are getting better and better" you can do that too.

You can do this. I know it.

XOXOXO

Affirmations that you may find helpful for the Index Card Assignment...

***all of these affirmations have been taken from various books written by my Mom, Toni Stone. In some cases they have been edited for use here.

- Today I am doubtless and sure.
- Today I do what I said I would do.
- Today I am capable of great things.
- I give up creating obstacles.
- I perfect new skills.
- I am avoiding what doesn't work.
- I rejoice in the company of good friends.
- I have happy holidays with my family.
- There is plenty to spare and share.
- Friends encourage me to achieve and I am grateful for them.
- Gratitude grows.
- Blessings are bountiful.
- Correct solutions are put into action.
- Divine ideas inspire action.
- I am a helper.
- Everybody helps someone else today.
- Families are grateful for each other.
- Forgiveness continues.
- Gladness is expressed.
- Miracles abound today.
- Good humor prevails.
- Great opportunities open up.
- Grief turns to gratitude.
- Happy actions happen.
- Inner wisdom grows.
- Kindness continues to occur.
- Laughter is let out.
- Life is lived joyfully.
- Limited thinking dissolves.

- Loving people occurs more often.
- Mistakes are cleaned up.
- Money multiplies.
- Motives are made pure.
- Negotiation brings solution.
- New goals are generated.
- Old makes way for new.
- Partnerships are based on truth.
- People listen and learn.
- People teach what they are learning.
- Praise prevails.
- Refreshing solutions become clear.
- Safety prevails.
- Skills bring benefit.
- Sparkling spirit shines forth.
- Teachings guide more good.
- Divine ideas are seen.
- Thinking differently enables much.
- Transformation continues.
- What matters is clear.
- What is false falls apart.
- What is hidden is revealed.
- Willingness to cooperate escalates.
- Wisdom is shared.
- I am fortunate, successful, and grateful.
- I know what to do and I do it.
- I know where to go and I go there.
- I know what to remember and I think of it.
- I know that giving causes getting…the more I give the more I get.
- I see what I decide to see.
- I change the way that I think about things.
- I only speak about the good.

- I have a future unlike the past.
- I always have what is necessary in each moment.
- I look to my future happily knowing that only the best comes to me.
- I have an attitude of gratitude.
- I produce what is new now.
- I expect only good.
- I remember only the good.
- Good is flowing in ever increasing amounts.
- What is required is always present.
- I am grateful that daily supply is abundant.
- I recognize the goodness and plenty of life.
- Today, I give up talking about problems.
- I am glad to see the highest good in all situations.
- I remember that whatever I talk about, I get more of.
- I change my speaking to reflect only what I want more of.
- I am learning new habits and behaviors now.
- I understand how everything can be used to bring about more good…I have that power…I use it.
- I know how to achieve intended outcomes.
- I easily manifest my goals.
- Seeming problems are diffused.
- Workable patterns emerge now.
- My good appears all over the place now.
- I am filled with JOY.
- I am happy, healthy and have plenty of energy to do what needs doing today.
- I spread joy.
- I accomplish great things with ease.
- I am glad to be cheerful and certain.
- I move beyond where I thought I was stuck.
- I identify with good ideas.
- I stop complaining.
- Good is abundant.

- I pay attention.
- My success is progressive.
- I open up pathways to new futures unlike the past.
- I am safe and protected wherever I go.
- I say goodbye to fear.
- I wake up alive and alert each morning.
- I am open and receptive to miracles in my day.
- I greet the day with optimism.
- I declare that fear has no power over me.
- Good is assured.

About the Author:

Noelle Federico is the owner of Fortunato Partners, Inc., a boutique consulting & marketing firm. She is a social media influencer and the creator of The Working Single Mom brand which has a reach of 24 million people monthly. She writes, teaches, speaks, consults, and coaches. Previously she spent 14 plus years as CFO, CMO and Business Manager of Dreamstime.com LLC, where she was a member of the founding team that created the global stock photography leader. Her focus has now returned to consulting, writing, coaching and project management. She spends a fair amount of time these days as the Director of Project Management for the Bryn Law Group in Miami, FL.

Noelle has over 3 decades of Executive experience across a number of different industries and has worked in numerous roles within corporate finance, operations, and communications.

She teaches Branding and Marketing and is the author of 'Notes on Branding' and several other books including 'Practical Change... 8 Ways to Rejuvenate Your Life' and 'Practical Change...Inspiration for Kicking Ass & Slaying Dragons.   She is also the Founder of the non-profit, A Generous Heart, Inc.

Noelle graduated from Fisher College in Boston, MA and also attended Suffolk University. Additionally, she is a graduate of the Dale Carnegie Training and a Landmark Worldwide graduate.
Formerly of Boston/ Cape Cod, MA and Franklin, TN ...she now resides in Fairfax, Vermont. She lives with her husband , two large cats and one small cat.

She is always happy to hear from you, you can reach her at:
noelle@fortunatopartners.com

and you can find her here:

https://theworkingsinglemom.com/
https://www.facebook.com/thewrkingsinglemom/
https://twitter.com/wrkingsinglemom
https://www.instagram.com/wrkingsinglemom/
https://www.pinterest.com/wrkingsinglemom/
https://www.linkedin.com/in/noelle-federico/
https://www.youtube.com/channel/UCrzzyjoZzGklhInsRb4flpg?reload=9
http://www.revealingexcellence.com/
https://www.facebook.com/revealingexcellence/

Noelle's Mother, Toni Stone passed away on Aug. 26th, 2020. A new website showcasing Toni's books among other things is under construction www.wonderworksstudio.com --- meanwhile you can visit her old site at www.wonderworks.org. If you are interested in purchasing any books available there please email noelle directly and she will assist you. Soon Toni's work will be available on amazon.com.

www.ingramcontent.com/pod-product-compliance
Lightning Source LLC
Chambersburg PA
CBHW081019040426
42444CB00014B/3278